1979

PERMISSION TO SPEAK

The Wesleyan Poetry Program : Volume 90

PERMISSION
TO SPEAK

POEMS BY
Steve Orlen

Wesleyan University Press
MIDDLETOWN, CONNECTICUT

Grateful acknowledgment is made to the following publications, in which some of these poems have appeared: *Agenda, The American Poetry Review, The Antioch Review, The Ardis Anthology of New American Poetry, Blue Moon News, The Face of Poetry, Field, Five Arizona Poets, The Iowa Review, Ironwood, Mazagine, The Mississippi Review, The New American Review, Poets of the Rio Grande, Poetry, The South Shore Review*.

Some of the poems in this collection appeared in two limited edition chap-books: *Sleeping On Doors*, Penumbra Press, Lisbon, Iowa, 1975; and *Separate Creatures*, Ironwood Press, Tucson, Arizona, 1976.

I am grateful to Jon Anderson, Mark Halperin, and Boyer Rickel, for their encouragement, and for their help in completing these poems. I would also like to thank the National Endowment for the Arts for a grant which allowed me time to work on some of these poems.

Library of Congress Cataloging in Publication Data

Orlen, Steve, 1942–
    Permission to speak.

    (Wesleyan poetry program; v. 90)
    I. Title.
PS3565.R577P4   811'.5'4   77–89038
ISBN 0–8195–2090–X
ISBN 0–8195–1090–4 pbk.

Manufactured in the United States of America

First Edition

For Gail, and for my friends, Spot & the Grommet,
Mark & Bobbi, Tina Feingold, John
Augustus Murphy, & Boyer Rickel

friends
Are so enclosed within my reasoning
I am occasionally them.

CONTENTS

SLEEPING ON DOORS

Carol Marcus 1946–1969

If we could only see further
We could look through to the other side.
Such impossibilities, the death of a sister

In August, leave us standing
In a kingdom of tongues
Without mouths, without even silence
To contain our doubts.
When we sigh we encounter her breathing.

To each ghost we assign lamentations
Like zeroes, like seeds.
We would people whole accessible universes
With our need; entrances, exits.

As if we could accept loss forever —

Tonight is the first closed door,
The stone, and we lie down on it, sleep
On the door, on the door, sleep on the door —

A way of seeing past the darkness,
As though we could come and go as we pleased.

I.

*"What a lot of needles there are, Malte, and how
they lie about everywhere, and when you think
how easily they fall out . . ."*
— Rilke, from *The Notebooks
of Malte Laurids Brigge*

UKRAINIAN PASTORAL

from a photo of my grandparents

On a wooded hillside by a river, a woman pauses
To catch her breath, leans against a silver birch.
What she sees we can't know, for her eyes are shut.
She is stocky, young; her calves glisten in sunlight.
When she opens her eyes to admit us, the earth
Is a maypole around which she sweeps a clearing.

Upon the water, a small boat is making its way
Toward shore, a man rowing, his muscular shoulders
Propelling him through mist. Perhaps he envisions
This shape on the hillside, who might be a wife
Or a sweetheart, waiting. But his back is to us.
Perhaps he shuts his eyes to hear the river's pulse.

When I enter the parlor, I think you've been reading
The book on your lap, but your eyes are shut.
I remove my old coat. I see a parakeet preening
In its cage, and a salad of onion and cucumber
Set on a table by a vase of yellow iris.
Was it something you heard, my foot on the walk,

That woke you? Or does light convert us into people,
Husband and wife, the one reading, the other
Entering an arch as he does each day of his life?
On the wall, a woman partially hidden by trees,
And a man gliding over water, about whom we can
Invent a story, or better, say nothing and wait.

NAMING THE CHILDREN

He remembers *good night* and *good morning.*
He remembers my wife, Gail, *which is the wind,*
Who sits beside him, stroking his thin right hand.

From back of the car through the neighborhoods
He recites the names of his children
In Russian, Hebrew and English. The names squeeze through

The damaged arteries, past the house in Odessa
Over the remarkable ocean to New York.
Mischa will be *Morris. Hodya* will be *Ida.*

Ten years later my mother, Beatrice Florence,
Stares into polished stone. At last
She sees herself, nee Bryna Fagel, *beautiful bird.*

Which is how it is in America,
Over the graves of our parents, how we are named.

Thick snow, the path, an evergreen
Hung above an ice-locked stream.
Home through the woods he found
A hand thrusting up from the snow.
His dog growled. The hand was frozen blue.
He was afraid to tell his father
Whom he told all his secrets, afraid
To touch the stiff, curled fingers
Or enter the cave of palm; but numb
With winter he came back to sit
In the widening circle of story:
A man lay by a northern stream,
Lost in trout-depths, feverish.
His gashed leg refused to heal.
That night the wolf returned to snarl.

Sunday when the others knelt in church
He pressed the blue fire of palm
And bound their hands in prayer.
He passed out in the snow.
The tree let down its branches
Over a boy who could not stay away
From the dead, or the soon to be dead,
And an owl from a story book sang
Of another world, the underground:
It snowed, and the stream froze up,
And dark clouds hid the stars.
In his dream they were friends,
Wolf and man, under a shell of dark.

Far off in the upper world
The miraculous living moved.
Nothing ended but the day.
A father storied his son to sleep;
Children woke and went to school.

The boy moved through them, a ghost,
Counting the unborn nails of his hand.
Cold voices urged him back to the woods.
Under the tree, a story was ending:
And when he died, steam rose
From his flesh, the wolf moaned
And ran, the body slipped under snow.

Then spring, and the snow loosed
Over rock to unveil a man's body.
He watched them wrap it in a sack
And saw that the eyes were blind,
The mouth too dumb for grief or story.
But their hands had locked, friends
One whole winter, until the stream broke
And blessed him with its cold skill.
He heard icy veins roaring underground.
He didn't know the dead could live
So long, nor pain, nor numbness end.

THE SIAMESE TWINS

Out the door, a hand or arm,
A swift look tells which one:
Fat one, thin one, shadow and light,
They float from sunlight to shadow,
And the boy, the new boy
Is confused: *Which one?* Two nearly
Identical faces lean over
An oaken table. Thin one has a fugitive charm,
Skittering off to the bathroom.
Fat one knits a scarf of winter blue
And white. Invited to sit
Or stand, he sips a cup of tea.

Two faces reason from the steam.
They are . . . they are two of them
So much he loses count.
Both are breathless
Beholding the new, shiny coin
From his coin collection and the frayed
Sneakers from his paper route, their eyes
Penetrate and won't let go.

In the other world, his twin
Is doing a phantom dance, a silver thing.

The poster on the wall above
The fireplace presents
A circus time, a story time:
Two goddesses emerge as steam
From a green lake dotted with islands —
The original lovely things.
His wish: to come upon them
Naked on the beach, pine-shadows
Mingle their pairs of breasts,

They tremble because they are
Surprised once more, beheld . . .

They are, his mother says, the famous
Gibb Sisters seen as a child in Atlantic City,
"They were so pretty then . . ."

They sat, over tea, and chatted.
He'll never remember what was said.
But pictured them trying
To swim a lake, two naked
Identical ladies, angry at each
Other, swimming toward a different
Island on which was a shack,
A cache of coins, a miserable strip of beach.

When you walked downstairs
And touched my root, God knows
What brought you homing there,
Barely fourteen, already known
As the town pump and proud
Of your clear attributes.
With breasts like new clouds,
You were my first, fallen angel.
I don't think we ever kissed,
But lay in a rocky ditch
All one awful summer night,
Alive, in love with heat.
At dawn we toasted marshmallows,
And when the fire caught
The weeds and lit the hillside,
You held me tight and whispered,
"Let's wait and see the fire
Engines come!" You got sent up early
To *The House of Good Shepherd*
Because the mothers were jealous,
Forgive them. When the friendly
Leering cop told me, "I heard
You dipped the wick in Beverly,"
I blushed and stammered, proud.
Then lied, forgive us all,
To save my skin. Beverly,
The night they took you away
I imagined myself in the ditch,
My flesh on fire, curled against
Your careless breathing,
Plotting love. I dreamt
Your face, and your hands
That parted the dark, were mine,
And groaned to share your misery,
But I found mine in good time.

TOBACCO FARMS

Under acres of white net I crawl
On my knees and worry about God
And sex and death. Sometimes I'd like
To lie in the damp row and dream,
But this is piecework, thirteen
Cents a bend, so I pick and think
And tender these delicate leaves.
Heat blazes under the nets
But mornings the dew is cool. At lunch,
The straw boss brings beer. I watch
The Polish immigrant, nose
In a grammar book, who arrived
Last week in a suit. By now
He's learned the vocabulary of fuck
This and fuck that.
                  On the truck ride
Home I dream of Bab's Beach, a dance
With the Pennsylvania girls. I'll
Drink, maybe fight. I'll watch
Stars wheel over the curing barns.
Meanwhile, Ace Cody's got a
New tattoo and the fat kid jiggles
His breasts like a woman. Monday,
Another field, the same river
Of nets all the way to the sea.
Not yet fourteen, and my
Father says I know too much.

BEAUTY AND THE BEAST

"Let me in." The four-year-old
  In printed dress and rubber boots
  Knocks on the door in the white woods.
  A jackrabbit scurries
  Across the roof of snow
  And hides behind the rotted oak.
  The coyote, lion and half-blind
  Dumb wild pig remain asleep inside.
  All this occurred before the dream
  Of a girl turned into a beast:
  The pink scar tensing the mouth
  In a permanent grin of aftermath,
  The one, wide-open, improbable eye.
"But it's only a dream," she cries,
"And couldn't happen to a Princess."

  Though it was afternoon, I slept,
  And whatever takes place in my dream
  I am faultless and a child again.
  The mother watches from the window,
  Idly watering flowers. And the large
  Black stubborn dog, mounting his mate
  On an endless ladder, for him
  This is a dream twice-yearly
  Of the maddening odor of bitch
  Into which he strides, he growls.

"Let me in," says the Princess.
  The dream's unlocked teeth
  Plunge into her face: the face
  In the window, the face in the dream
  Ripped half-off like a door from its hinge;
  Blood rushing from the bared skull
  Onto the dream of snow

Over which she trudges crazily home:
"Up horsie! Whoa horsie, whoa!"

There is no horse, no Princess,
No beast from fairy tales,
Only a dog dreaming of bullets
Raining down like bad weather
And a man slamming a car door.
At the dream's end, she whispers
"Let me in," and I wake, sweating,
In a room with a strange, one-eyed
Improbable Princess by my side.

COUNTRY HOUSE

This house is old, too small to contain
Lives furnished with smog, tv, divorce.
The trees I drag like errant children
From the hills are squandered in the fireplace.

The coyotes howl at nothing, a fiction,
A household in the woods. This antique bed
Would rot in some garage, but for my sentiment.
Gullies without pipes, land without the small dots

Of houses cozy in tracts, waste their scars.
We are the new outlanders, here for rest
And a taste of our fathers' blood. We gorge
On fresh, up-country air, breed violent flowers

Whose incessant odor frightens and consoles.
I imagine my father in this house, child
Of heartstruck immigrants, dreaming of hard work
And a fast buck. He stands on a street corner

In a shally hat and knickers hustling papers
Under a gas lamp. Whose past does he romanticize —
The sour smell of pigs, a Russian slum?
No gain in that. Why do we love what's gone?

The innocence we enshrine in sepia
Of Sunday picnics on the Dnieper is equal
To our own false lives, greed and deceit.
Therefore, we live small in a country house

And send out vines. When autumn comes
We crush the plump fruit into wine,
Drowse by the fire, and pump our children full of a past
That was sweet, a future ruined before their time.

II.

PERMISSION TO SPEAK

for Norman Dubie

Mornings, from my upstairs window, I can see a gray
Stand of birch and further down a hickory grove,
Then the river that powers the mill that grinds flour.
Later, I'll eat the bread. Last night a spring snow
Blurred the countryside, and for a while I lost my way.

I thought I saw a boy in a crimson bathing suit
Whirl downstream on an inner tube; so I closed my eyes
On the old words for *birch* and *hickory* and *snow*
Like a novice in his cell discovering light,
Not the *One,* but another about which he'll remain
Silent all his life. I came to myself at the window.

That boy, already seen in memory, gives me permission to speak.
After a spring snow a father and son took a sleigh ride
Along the riverbank; and what the son couldn't see —
The particular hills and trees lost to whiteness —

Made him cry. The father snapped the reins, and pointed at
What must have been a red fox sliding past a birch:
"Look at that fellow in the bright nightgown!" From which
The son will date his love of the world, traveling swiftly past.

27

THE SOLACE OF POETRY

Is not the solace of gossip, though I can guess
Particulars of your life. Often from my
Window seat I watch two neighbors —
Breast, cheek and flank, that wilderness —
And something glowing in the dark like
A string of pearls from one mouth to the other.

As a child I wanted to be everyone. I spied
On the man delivering milk, and on his counterpart
In striped pajamas at his kitchen table,
Thinking himself alone while the world slept.
Your poems say hello. It's private: the child's
Need to both keep and share a secret

After the lamp is off. I lay your book aside
To watch the old couple undressing before sleep.
They examine each scar and mark in the body's
History. Something enters their life like water
Enters a pond at night, lies in their bed, faceless as a doll
Beneath the quilt's remembered weight, and does not speak.

THE BIPLANE

for Rolly Kent

Sometimes the night is not enough. I rise remembering,
And the dream is no longer a quaint story
In another's life, but my own grown more real.
Last night a biplane landed in my neighbor's field.
I watched, from my window seat, the canvas wings
Graze the rows of corn and come to rest.
                                     Afternoons
Seem always time between the crests of dream. There is
An oak outside my window so stunted, its limbs
Elbowing this way and that, it seems it had made
A decision not to grow beyond its needs. In spring
The leaves appear, in fall they yellow and curl,
And I know the constant change in direction is a
Ruse to make it seem more humble.
                                   Again last night
The biplane landed in my neighbor's field.
It caught fire, but when the wind finally blew
It out, I felt like the child who snuffs a match
In a closet and finds himself alone and bodiless.
Just think: I forgot the dream today. I woke
And drank my coffee, washed, put on my clothes;
On the way to work, I stopped and turned back,

But couldn't think what it was I had forgotten.
It was like the biplane from World War I.
Beyond the window, the tree was waving its arms.
A pilot from long ago, wearing my father's cap
And goggles, was waving his arms. Now I remember.
It was my father's dream, told to me as a child,
Put on like a coat that one day fits. I rise from
My window seat. Remember the child who wanted never
To grow up? The child has gone and found his way.

29

UNWRITTEN LETTERS

for Gerald and Jon

This is one of those letters I meant to write
While shaving or walking the dog. It always begins
Dear Brother, or *Dear Friend.* When I was a child
I wrote things down and sewed the words into sleeves,
Thoughts like clouds that changed when I watched them.
I buried them with the bottlecaps, the matchbooks,
In the backyard under the elm. I meant to dig them up.

Years later I think: our lives change ceaselessly;
How much older we have grown. If I write this letter
This is how you'll remember me: the curtains shut,
The sun going down, the cells of my body stopped.
I must have been thinking of you, of all we've said
Or left unsaid; of all the things we meant
To do. There is nothing that I meant to say.

There's a mirror right above my desk. When I look up
There I am. The eyes drift. My face has lost
Its symmetry. The two halves live separately.
Is this what happens to people alone? I'm afraid,
When you see me again, my face will suffer its parts
Unequally; one side will limp after the other,
Always the younger brother, unable to catch up.

When I look in the mirror, sometimes I see your face:
The eyes unfocused, settled within. The mouth says
Nothing now, content to wait. If we reached out
To touch one another, we would find the glass dark
And getting darker. To bring the two together
Requires patience, tact. My face is like the life I lead.
I meant to say, I'm doing fine. I can't describe it.

WHITE NIGHT

Earlier I had the son's recurring nightmare. The room
In which I stood was darkening; gradually the face
In the mirror broadened into my father's: the hair
Receded over a cup-white brow; the round, diminishing eyes
Held back, blinked, and blinked again. I woke to a loneliness
I couldn't grieve or understand. Part of me turned away.

Someone turns on a faucet, someone opens a door.
My mother stands on the lawn, wearing a white nightgown.
She was reading a novel and lost the thread of her story.
I've got the grown son's tic. *Mother, I'd like your consent.*
As she stares at the moon, a small creature huddles
So close to her ankles he must not know she's there.

It's true we have things in common, and memory is a suckler
That takes what it can get. Over my coffee cup
I imagine a child so thin light passes through him
As he walks to the bathroom. Someone will hold his hand.
Once I would have taken my mother's hand and led
Her to bed, and had a long conversation
On the day's events, waiting for the snow to stop.

But now she seems like a saint, so obsessed she might
Create a miracle. She watches a blind
Baby mole rush in circles at her feet, having lost
The tunnel that winds for miles under the lawn.
For a moment I've entered his confusion — a world of light
Just beyond his reach — a kind of exhalation
That I resolve into a mingling of identity and regret.

BEING MARRIED

> *"You have painted evening, a sense*
> *Of marriage, but not of being one."*
> — Pamela Stewart

I.

You sat with your parents
On a porch and watched the rose of Sharon
Shed its light at dusk; beyond, a double row
Of birches and the road that runs between.

What else can you talk about but restraint
Of evening, the outline of the trees
Extending branches toward the city?
You watched the fireflies disappear. Your father

Whispered how short life is, and your mother,
Handkerchief to mouth to stop the bleeding
Of a tooth, was careful not to interrupt . . .

Not light, but darkness coming on. The moon
Drew you from this yard down the row of birches —
A double error — from which there would be no return.

2.

The birchwood frame legitimizes. The painting:
You, at table, reading a book over
A checkered cloth, a pot containing some jam.
Your wife, the painter, taps to say she's sorry,
Please, one moment more. On her brush-tip,

A pale blue. A vein throbs
In your right forearm, but no one will care:
This is an intimate stranger
Gazing at blue that swims through his hands.
Behind him, along a riverbank, fields of goldenrod.

The painter specks in swallows darting for fireflies.
On his forearm, a tattoo of a swallow in flight.
This is called *Being Married,* though he sits alone.

3.

Lately marriage falls into friendship,
Two people posing in an earthly light.
What came between them was a child
Born from household language. The child

Has wandered for hours between rooms
Down the corridor that divides this house.
He's found an imaginary playmate, *Carol,*
Because the prettiest name in a library book . . .

The painter returns from coffee. The sun
Gone down, fishermen string out
Lights on the river. From the painter's robe,
One breast and its aureole peek out.

How to put off adulthood just a little more.
If she keeps painting, she'll figure it out:
How light transforms this scene
If she's not watchful; how the man, the painted man

At table dreams of a swallow bringing the worm
Glistening to a nest in the trees
That overhang the house. The swallow almost drops the worm.

4.

During the fifteen hours from rising
To sleeping, days, weeks, years
Eclipse according to the small events:

The cupboard mouse, the 2 a.m. train whistle.
Your face in the river is water, a picture.
A mouth or eye emerges. The moon's fragments comb your hair.

The child exists in the husband's dream.
The dreamer, a kidnapper, bears over the house
Harvest of all that is good in the house,

The oldest error.

THE BEST HALVES OF OUR LIVES

The dark lake's emptiness spreads to its receding shores.
The last red flag of day breaks down, and I look back
And dream, patient for miracles. I'm glad to be alone
To evoke your images around a table playing cards,
Old friends with little to say. At our feet the dogs
Sleep fitfully. Our wives, who keep us together
And apart, rise to remind us of our daily lives.

I stand by the water watching clouds; for whole days
Remember nothing at all. Here at the edges
Less matters. I measure life by seasons away
From friends, imagining each in his storybook house
Writing letters which ascend with their secrets
Toward silence and settle miles away on my roof.

And the angel in the lake, imperfect friend, finds me
In this other place, grim with maturity and distance,
Watching a kingfisher and a swallow dip in a last
Evening flight, and meet their shadows rising in the water.

I I I.

But I identify myself, as always,
With something that there's something wrong with,
With something human.

— Randall Jarrell

THE DRUNKEN MAN

There's nothing you can say to a man who drinks.
He rises in the gray mist of morning and lights
His cigarette, knowing that soon he'll be elsewhere.
Out in the world the old men sweep their shops
And one barber nods. The full-breasted woman
Airing her pillows, she smiles and squints,
And seeing it is only him, she closes the window.
But it doesn't matter. There's no way of hurting
A man who drinks. His wife floats in his pockets.
His father twists open the cap. His mother whispers
Drink, drink. He moves on down the street.

There are times when I feel obligated to speak.
I take my hands from my pockets.
I slide my glass away from him. In earnest
I'll say something — anything, the weather . . . my son —
And he'll argue at me from some place
I can't know because I'm not a drunk.
Perhaps when I stagger home my wife screams
To shut up, come to bed like a man. My face
Reddens, my shoes drop, I burrow into her flesh.

But a drunk is like a cloud, is like a ship
That sinks but never drowns, is like a feather bed.
Already it is noon. His mother and his father
Are half gone. He's weightless now.
I shouldn't waste pity on a drunken man. At night
In the bar I am his weakness, his hope,
And his family. If I argue back,
If I arm-wrestle him, if the bartender
Is embarrassed by my antics, it's time to go home.
Go home. Go home to my noisy wife.

STREETFIGHTER

Steve Ferreira 1949–1976

Last night two young Chicanos called him out,
Flat and simple as a threat of rain.
He tells me how his streetwise mind imagined
Left arm cocked, elbow a greased socket;
How he rose from the barstool and left.
Now he stops at the corner. His moon-
Face shrinks in the sun with worry.
When a friend confesses cowardice
It is an act of faith, and anything can happen.
I become a mouth to blame, mouth to forgive,
Mouth to explain that nothing matters.

I want to tell him, Age gives us courage
To deny some fool's left hook, bad night.
But what's the use? At twenty-five,
He still slicks his hair back like a hoodlum.
He turns and waves. Where we grew up
A good fight was a way of keeping friends,
And anything could happen. But if I run
Toward him and hit him in the mouth,
It would be one punch too few. I believe
He must go easier for trusting me his shame,
And worse for having begun this day
The wrong way twice. Dumb with rage
He prowls the avenues, will not be denied.

THE LAST WHORE

Red lights waken La Perla at the island's edge.
Along the sea wall, cold-eyed sharks in business suits
Lean and advise. These are the tourists' tropics
Where love swarms and the women are flowering out
Of every door. Upstairs in the Rose of Lima
Two lesbians fondle on stage in a velvet bed.
Their breasts are purple bruises spreading over
The sailors and cruising girls. Lily, the black
Dominican, flares across the room. A man waits.
Tattooed spiders clamber up her thighs. They talk
And drink, bargain and refuse, until she is soft,
Approximate, turning the way his hands turn
Like a block of wood on a lathe.
                                    Given the right word
Or the whim, or whatever moves us to break faith
With what we know, she might walk out and settle
On the outskirts of Ciudad Trujillo, proprietress
Of bar or beauty shop, and the man go home to a loving
Daughter, a loving wife. And yet as she turns,
The right word is a shape they do not speak.
Just under the sheet the last name chosen from a field
Of flowers steals his breath, and pushes him past
The spider gate. He is the last of many to enter
The wide, accustomed dark. They drift on the bed
Toward dawn, the last man and the last whore going down
Like the moon over La Perla, until they sleep or drown.

THE SECRET

I left a Mexican coin to confuse her. I left it
In the drawer with her mementoes: letters to
And from the dead, the oval portrait of her sister.
Love must keep its secrets, but not its hidden
Things. After dinner, I slid the brass coin in
Among the seeds and the lush flesh of a watermelon.
It disappeared, the lover's version of a magic
Trick to resurrect mysterious strangers.

Love must keep its secrets, between bathroom
And kitchen, and in the marriage chamber.
We try to sleep. In a dream, she finds the coin
Wedged between her breasts. Lovely in my bed,
She dreams of other men and unfamiliar places.
By morning she needs a bus trip. She's bored.
I know. I left a Mexican coin to distract her
From love and its mischief, eyes making eyes

At strangers as we pass. Across the aisle
I watch her finger it in her bluejeans pocket,
Smooth it, make it lucky. Such wearing down
Takes years. The bus stops in Mexico City.
We lie together, two strangers in a painted bed.
We hardly know each other well enough, she whispers,
To undress in this humid dark. Stars drift
Above the skylight. The hours pass. I think
I am falling in love with the need for fictions.
The coin glows between us. The coin knows.

THE PERFECT ONE

My friend tells me I don't understand women,
A good question to ask myself in private.
Consider my suicides, my wives, who gave birth
To me daily. Under their wings I was slick
And charming. They were the coddlers who kept me.
To the shadows of their breasts I brought my grief.
But the man, the elusive one, hid his eyes and slept.

Consider the advice my mother gave me
Wheezing on her knee: "Never marry a girl
Who can't sing in your sleep." I never did.
I couldn't find her. I lay awake.
"A boy takes wives by being forcefully inept,
A man steps into a woman's life by being blunt."
But Mother's gone the way of most perfection
And Father turned out to be right after all.
When I was crazy I touched a tree.
I asked it what it was, beyond itself.
I think I suffered a long time without knowing.

In the mornings a lady comes to rouse me.
She is not my lover, she is not my mother.
She is the future and she is desperate to please me.
When she hands me my toothbrush, I tell her,
"Wait, you are the Perfect One, I can see
Right through you." In the next bed my father writes,
"Everything will happen in its time . . ."

I had a dream last night in which
She came for me. "I'm not ready," I said,
But she was all smiles like the bark of a tree.
As I grew smaller, she grew more perfectly large.
Then she found it, my birthmark, and entered
My body through that one remaining hole without teeth.
"Get out," I told her, "you're just like me!"

43

She smelled like death as I breathed her out.
All of this is written in the book my father wrote.

If an angel had a face, fishermen
Would want something ugly
Like the boy who hawks
Souvenirs on the docks.
Face disfigured from birth,
Mouth slung open at harbor
And sky, and the eyes tilted
Perpetually upward
Watch for white sails veering
In the wind, sailing home
To a face so familiar
The fishermen forgot.
                              God,
To this boy, is the postman
Who has no face, skin
Burnt to a thinness
The boy could almost
Read words through.
The postman passes the docks,
Striding from business to
Business like the tides,
And in his bag
Letters from the poor,
From the children
Begging for more.

The Devil can mold his face
To any shop window
The boy looks into after dark.
The street is hushed.
The Devil comes running when
The postman's not delivering
And the fishermen are drinking
Because no fish have been caught
All day. The Devil

Is faster than the boy
Can run, even now as he waits
Out of breath to be taken.

LAST LIGHT

for Tina F.

Before picking up the knife, I stared out the window
At the street, neutral, dull, until a woman passed
Leading a funny red dog. Her lips pursed
In a whistle I could not hear. Just one kiss,

I thought, through her belly to the bones
And the organs barely kept in place.
I held my breath. The woman turned the corner
And I opened the window to follow the trill

Over the red roofs. Some last light
Caught the knife's blade — caught up
Its strength — and quivered three times.
All the others in the city, I thought,

Walk off their murders with their little dogs
And I sit by the window taking notes.
Something went wrong. I was left numb, a brain
Blind in a damp cell far from the heart.

THE MADMAN'S WIFE

The unleashed dog walks back and forth. The cat
Leaps over the backyard fence. The owl
Shifts. Down this street the madman threads his way
Over curb and cobblestone and does not fall.
At dawn everyone smiles. The butcher has saved
The plumpest hen for him. The barber trims his hair.
The children tease him because he is there,
Less than a child, more than a lump. Later he sits
Across from me at breakfast, talking of suicide.
His plate becomes the tin plate prisoners use
To rattle their complaints. Last night in a bar, he says,
A woman disguised as a wife told him lie after lie.

There's no way to answer, so I put him to sleep.
What does he dream with his eyes open? I might
As well ask what a child dreams before speech
Gives him the power to lie. Out the window
The dog sees the shadow of the cat. The cat looks
After the owl. The owl keeps the moon in place.
To be mad, I know, is to be out of touch with life;
To touch a stranger in a bar and say, *My wife.*
But even the truth would be a betrayal. He wakes.
Read me a story, he begs, *tell me the names.*
I gaze into his white eyes, into the blue gas
Swirling in his heart. *Oh, poor us,* I begin.

IV.

INSTRUCTIONS FOR PAINTING A CORPSE: A LECTURE

after Cennini

You must not use rosy tints, for a dead man's flesh
Is like the oldest gardener's coat at dusk

In a rainy country. Portraiture, like gardening,
Is the art of the solitary who keeps long hours

For nothing to do, and the rose is an afterthought.
Mark the boundaries, mix with a little black

Which is called *sanguigno*. Place in sunlight to dry.
It is good to sit with the corpse while waiting:

In the Orient disciples of a Master will
Flock around his deathbed for instructions, as around

A candle flame that in its dying light
Will sputter, then leave us to our lives.

In life, this was Giovanni the gardener
Who was kindly to all and lived temperately. See how

The lines of the mouth
Pursue a man even past Death's Gate. Therefore,

Paint the bones of Christians or rational creatures
With the same devotion.

Paint the hair, not so it shall appear alive,
But without the sheen the head's oil puts forth. Each strand,

As in the blaze and mane and tail of a horse,
Must be accounted for. Men with active and clear minds

Become sentimental at the news of death,
But not at death's *body,* which is chaste

Like a doll's. Those who converse with dolls,
Or with the dead, earn the right to be alone.

To set the corpse apart, use a drapery of violet,
Blue or red: to be loved or tolerated,

As you would a visiting niece from the Capitol
Who must be sat in a corner for upsetting her milk

Or for weeping at odd moments. Make the face
As uniform as snow, the cold bloom of a painter's mistress,

Before whom he quails, and must choose to die
Of that sinless hunger

Or at last fall at her merciless feet and pray.
The mistress, the fair young niece, and the brown old gardener

Appear alike and are alike disagreeable in death. Each
Has a thin, transparent caul of skin

We call the *cuticula,* a little wet and thinner
In the maiden, but beneath which lies the fat

And lean and all the blood as under a sheet of ice.
This man, who was content to die stretched out

In the early morning shade of an olive tree,
Is content to lie in this approaching studio darkness.

On the subject of death we have no authority
Except this speechless corpse, whose last breath

Seems to flicker, as, now, dusk sinks into night.
All our futures depend upon such moments, without sentiment

Or artifice to save us.

THE PAINTER: A MEDITATION

The wandering jew's scarlet leaves hang in my space.
I like to think they're peaceful, but the air
Pulsates and shadows shrink from the vine. My eyes
Thread this space. My hands are in love with light.
The light is external, its passage from grief to grace.
I had wanted to make a picture of the world
Where nothing was for sale, where women walked down
To their gardens for solace, and a little light.

But people sit uneasily in spaces meant for objects.
I can't hold hands with a model whose face
Is dressed with light. When I take up the brush
I am not transformed, nor is time mitigated.
For a long time I meant to be depressed, a sudden
Jumping out of windows without goodbyes; now
I paint to stay alive. What mysteries may dwell
Where leaf and shadow meet, I'd rather not find words for,
Having their own reasons, as in the truth of fables.

Last night I tried to invent something impersonal
To save my life. Though it was hot, I pulled
The covers over me and lay in dream awhile. What I saw
Was a face so large I couldn't contain its grief. I heard
My children, curled in their little bags of sleep,
And their breathing calmed me, the way a winter storm
Keeps us from leaving the house. I wanted to invent a glacier
Of such crystalline purity that even the cleverest among us
Couldn't discover its flaw. Morning caught me unawares.

Look, I'm killing a shadow, instilling light
Where no light ought to be. Sometimes I forget
The world where floors are swept for a reason.
The insane begin by neglecting to clean, each morning,
Their faces in the mirror. There is proof:
There are photos of better days. None of my paintings

Poses any questions. Even the slow rise
Of a blue penis by the easel, even my husband
Who demands his breakfast and his morning touch —

Nothing human moves me. I watch the slow crawl
Of light up the wandering jew, deeper than flesh.
I listen to water dripping in the sink, and children
Pummeling each other in the schoolyard next door,
And I think only of flowers in a still life. A painter
Loves in unspeakable places, by hand and eye.
Such cannibalism is an emotion, a courtship of flesh.
This morning I started a still life of cups and saucers
Surrounded by a house, a small domestic scene.
I tried to paint the face. It never came out the same.

Nothing is sure or knowable, even these eyes
I call my own. A man walks in and out, dressed
With a bluish light. We say hello, like the wandering
Jew meeting the air, as though leaf and stalk, elbow
And bud, were expressions of our fear of life.
There are stories, but we are separate creatures
Who bruise each other when we pass. Lord,
I'd like some light, please.

The snippings of the wandering jew weave
Their filaments in a jar of fresh water. It eats
To stay alive. This morning the household sleeps,
Deep in the glacier's flaw. Its breathing
Keeps me from myself. It will carry me into my grave.
If God had a face I'd never be able to paint it,
It would be so large. Later I'll go down to the garden
And watch the ants pleasing their fat queen.

BLACK ON WHITE

1. *Black on White*

The two of us stood in snow
On the mountainside. You reached out,
And as I was meeting your hand
I saw you fall and begin

The long slide down a snow trough.
You disappeared into pines.
I stood a long time looking down,
Believing you dead, composing

Myself for a death. Such scenes
Are etched in the mind; they last
All winter, gazing over
A valley into a belt of pines.

I believe you fell to let me go.
I must have spoken your name,
But standing tired me and
Everywhere I looked I had to wait.

2. *Who Was I*

Who was I that I couldn't run
Through nets of syringa and sink
My teeth in the warm she-goat. *Cougar,*

We thought, because her neck was broken on the creosote.
"Don't look," my wife warned, knowing my fear
Of hurt things. Next day our neighbor shot

A yearling bear drinking our other goat.
I didn't see him skin, or take the meat
For thanks. All summer the question was

Who broke the net around our house and took
Two goats, who for two summers
Followed us on walks and gave us milk.

3. *Dusk*

The boy on the curb watches the line
Where shadow edges on pink. He's patient.
Last night he watched his brother thrash,
Dreaming a loud and masculine dream.
The boy could have stopped it, but didn't know when
To move, and he might have been dreaming
Himself. Today, swimming the storm drain, he felt
In himself the power to stop the water.

His brother woke, screaming. The water churned
Around the snagged branch of a lime tree.
Next time. He looks up as the ball drops
Toward the basket and shadow edges
The pink that washed his leg. He's not yet
Sure how to interfere with the world.

4. *Conception*

The bell that starts to ring —
We let it ring — goes on
Naming its small, diminishing hour,

Seed of a child some afternoon
Fixed there at the end of time.
We like to think a spirit

Intervened, its hand in ours,
Though we can't recall whether
We loved for this or that reason,

So gave, instead, a small, diminishing start
As the bell on the tower
Reminded us: *not how, but when.*

5. *The Genealogist*

When I open this carved stone and enter,
Nothing can be otherwise. The row of smelt
Hangs on the line across the yard from sheets,

And through the steam I watch an old woman
Clean the fish, and a man sharpen the knives.
When I squint, I can see the stonemason

Over his cunning tools. From that solitude
He carves the image of water and clouds
And a hanged man, the clouds worn like bandages

Over the restless eyes. When I can't remember
What I do with my days, I see a pocked face
Bent over a bench, mumbling, *Because of us.*

THE SAINT

In the heart of Umbria
Francis of Assisi was born.
His father owned a horse to take
The family through the countryside,
And when the boy saw a field mouse borne
Away in a hawk's claws, he felt as hard as the war
Extended over the gloomy
Highway away from Florence, to his grandmother's farm.
That night (this from his diary)

He watched the faces of his family in sleep,
And for the moment believed
He was the only one alive. He knelt
And poured his body into his knees on the floor.
Dreaming, he came on a red cottage
Down a hill toward a stream, and his eyes fixed
On a murder taking place inside —
The ritual of blood foaming out
Of a woman's side. From this he sought
A rational power too severe to satisfy.

So he grew and roamed.

With little love for priests
And the tired women who followed
Everywhere he walked, he allowed
Their watching of his ministrations to the animals.
He felt no nostalgia for the dead
(We see his mouth, often painted
Flower-like, equivocal),
For like a mother of too many
Children, his strength
Was a kind of disenchantment: he had no faith.

Complex with age, as if the severity
Of youth were preparation

For a death, he carried a lock
Of his grandmother's hair
On walks. Everywhere he heard
Echoes of himself, beating
Of too many tired hearts, and all paths away
From cities were fingers stripped
Of flesh. He tried to pass those fingers

Into the walls of his skull, but there
Was no escaping the huddled farmers
Who brought their sorry cows. Though it was said
He never loved any woman, he offered
The lock of hair as a token of his need; he
Always took it back. He told one disciple
He carried that memory of his family
In sleep, thinking them dead,
That the gray hair sprouting from the widow's
Peak oppressed him by its passion.

At his death, the whole country
Undulated. He was Fate: a lack
Of emotion in the fingertips. He became
The easiest of saints to sentimentalize.
Perhaps he was the invention
Of the religious painters, a gourd
Into which some country wine was poured.
We make from that wine some parables,
Not of ourselves, but of what we wish
To commemorate, moral in us all,
A kind of obligation, or human invention
Best left misunderstood.

SIX PERSIMMON

Gathered four or five hundred years ago in an orchard,
These six persimmon reflect a vague spire of water.
The orchard was tended by a girl with her robe undone.

The painter opened his window to copy the road,
And the girl who was crossing it (thinking herself unobserved):
That which passed, cloudy sky and the thin trees of autumn,

And that which came to pass: intoxication
Of the eye reflecting light on flesh, quiver of air
At the edge of the breasts. Painting is the cruelest art,

The disinterested truth inking her poor, flat hair;
And the portrait of a girl became an abstraction
Of a robe pressing inward on the milky breasts, which,

If released, would spoil this contemplative afternoon.
The artist may have known that beneath his own saffron
Robe was a desire whose quivering has just now ceased,

And his fingers, furtive a moment ago, launched forth
To ink out the curve of the breast and escape those open eyes
Which after many years will reappear as fruit here in America.

SELF-PORTRAIT

Certainly Velasquez saw these reflections:
The stained beards of saints after the god's death
And the holes in their faces declaring
How empty life can be before the end
With the tongues cut out, the children already born.

Down the hill in a savage monastery
My apprentice sits. We haven't yet made
Our communion, but he believes in me.
In the boredom of hard bread, and the delicate
Roots of his dinner, he says my name
Aloud to the walls. Out his window,

Over red sand and stone, a narrow stream
Of water makes its way. That young man
Must have seen enough: brilliant lights
Of the city at night, and the man kissing
Himself in the yellow window on the hill.

It's me in the window, the model for this
Portrait. I give myself shamelessly, I show
The hole of my mouth, my genitals;
An entire Spanish landscape snakes down
My belly. Still, we couldn't stop anyone
From dying or the sensitive from going mad.

When Velasquez's coffin was opened
Two skeletons were found holding hands,
But the skulls had turned aside. We live
In the heart of each hour, making refusals
Into art. Our childhoods — pure hills of grape
And wheat — were unhappy, and should have been
Left behind. Our paintings were mirrors:

Glassy skin, nothing but light in whose flame
A moth twisted and burned. Visions
In the moist cafes and nothing had to make sense.
We were honest, learning our craft, but traded
Love for ambition the way the poor
Trade seeds from the garden for buttons.

The gossips said we went out too often
In our rowboats, singing, that we drank
Too much light. Under the wide lindens
The heavy shadows begin to spread their fruit.
Younger men will find in those shadows
Grace in a green penumbra
Out of which something mortal begins to grow.